I AM
BLIND
AND
MY DOG
IS DEAD

Humor- Some of
it a little sick- perhaps-
to help you get well.
C & G

I AM BLIND
AND
MY DOG
IS DEAD

CARTOONS BY
S. GROSS

AVON
PUBLISHERS OF BARD, CAMELOT AND DISCUS BOOKS

I am indebted to the following copyright owners for permission to reprint cartoons owned by them:

Of the 117 drawings in this collection, 23 appeared originally in *The New Yorker* and were copyrighted © in 1973, 1974, 1975, 1976, and 1977 by The New Yorker Magazine, Inc. Cartoons on pages 16/17, 18, 26, 35, 51, 54 *bottom*, 58, 66, 71, 74, 76, 78, 80, 82/83, 95, 100/101, 104, 107 *bottom*, 110, 115, 120 *bottom*, and 124 appeared originally in *Ladies' Home Journal*. Copyright © 1969, 1970, 1971, 1972, 1973, 1975, 1976, and 1977 by Downe Publishing, Inc. Cartoons on pages 40 *bottom*, 48 *bottom*, 52/53, 56, 62, 79, 89, 91, 97, 106, 112, 127, and 128 appeared originally in *Saturday Review*. Copyright © 1965, 1966, 1967, 1969, 1970, 1971, 1972, 1974, and 1975. Cartoons on pages 12, 15 *top*, 32, 45, 46, and 72 appeared originally in *The New York Times*. © 1973/76 by The New York Times Company. Cartoons on pages 69, 98, 116, and 122 are reprinted from the August 1972, January 1970, October 1968, and May 1971 issues of *Good Housekeeping Magazine*. © 1968, 1970, 1971, and 1972 by the Hearst Corporation. Cartoons on pages 21, 30/31, 49, and 77 reprinted from *Audubon*, the magazine of the National Audubon Society. Copyright © 1975, 1976. Cartoon on pages 118/119 reprinted courtesy *Writer's Digest* magazine. © August 1975. Cartoon on page 126 reprinted courtesy 1976 Writer's Yearbook. © 1976. Cartoon on page 73 reprinted from The Saturday Evening Post. © 1965 The Curtis Publishing Company. Cartoon on page 38 © *The Washington Post*. Cartoon on page 44 © by the Chicago Tribune-New York News Syndicate, Inc. Cartoon on page 57 reprinted from the Summer 1975 *Barrister*. Copyright © 1975 by the American Bar Association. Cartoon on page 102 reprinted from TV GUIDE® Magazine. Copyright © 1976 by Triangle Publications, Inc. Radnor, Pennsylvania. Grateful acknowledgement is also made to the following publications in whose pages many of the cartoons reprinted in this book first appeared: *National Lampoon, McCall's, Private Eye, Esquire, Head, Cosmopolitan, Gourmet, True, Cavalier, Argosy,* and *The Critic*.
This book's first cartoon appears on page 9.

AVON BOOKS
A division of
The Hearst Corporation
959 Eighth Avenue
New York, New York 10019

Copyright © 1977 by S. Gross
Published by arrangement with Dodd, Mead and Company
Library of Congress Catalog Card Number: 77-7314
ISBN: 0-380-40162-2

First Avon Printing, September, 1978
Third Printing

AVON TRADEMARK REG. U.S. PAT. OFF. AND IN
OTHER COUNTRIES, MARCA REGISTRADA, HECHO EN
U.S.A.

Printed in the U.S.A.

For Isabelle

On Sam Gross

New Yorkers were enduring mid-July of 1936 while on the other side of the world, a little beyond the Ural Mountains, the famous Tumbling Putkovics had loaded their wagon, left Uvat, and headed North. They journeyed by moonlight several nights and one day pitched tent on the banks of the River Ob.

Uncle Sid Putkovic called little Sam to his knee and said, " 'Sweetie,' avoid milksops, stay clear of sneaks and don't ever marry an animal trainer!" Uncle Sid thought Sam was a girl. He was thrown off because of little Sam's gunny dress.

Ten years later at Ellis Island, New York, a clerk was unable to spell or pronounce Putkovic. The famous Tumbling Putkovics were then entered into the record as the Gross family.

Sam did well in the years to come. He avoided milksops. Rumor was, among New York cartoonists, that he had been seen in the company of a sneak one Wednesday — but no matter. He married well. Uncle Sid never understood the business Sam was in until cartooning was explained as manufacturing.

Nowadays Sam manufactures cartoons for *The New Yorker*, *National Lampoon*, and Sesame Street. He was the idea man behind "The Genius," an aborted comic strip, and recently completed two years as President of the Cartoonists Guild.

Sam's cartoons cause folk to snort, twitch and make strange noises. But these are noises of joy. A blind man begging with a tin cup while dragging his dead seeing-eye dog — that's a long way from the banks of the River Ob and little Sam's gunny dress.

George Booth

S. GROSS

"Hello. My name is Linda. I'm your bunny for the experiment today."

S.GROSS

"Any children?"

S. GROSS

"Who's behind this?"

"It's true. You were actually born a beautiful princess but you were given to us to be brought up . . . and there's not a damned thing you can do about it!"

"You are going to get the measles within the next two weeks."

S.GROSS

"This one wasn't planned."

"I told you never to try a somersault."

S. GROSS

"On second thought, I don't want the responsibility."

"Sorry. Next!"

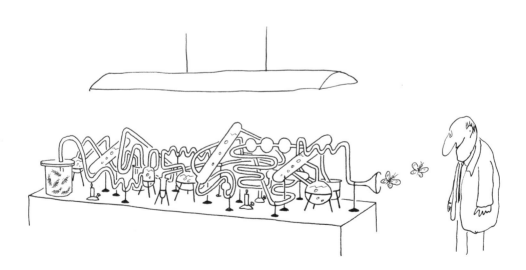

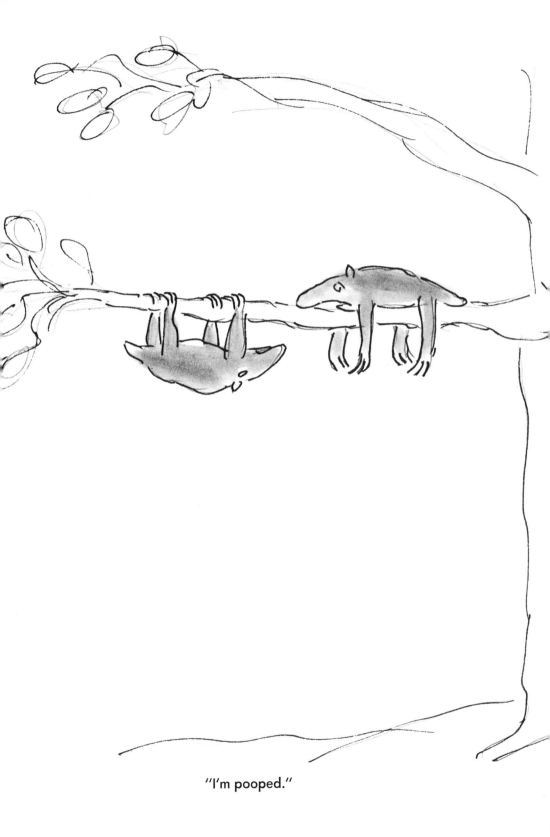

"I'm pooped."

S. GROSS

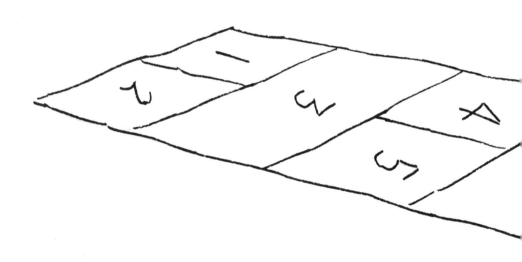

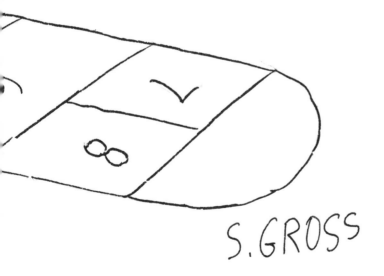

S. GROSS

"I'm a Cheshire mouse."

"They got me, Lennie. I'm wounded."

S. GROSS

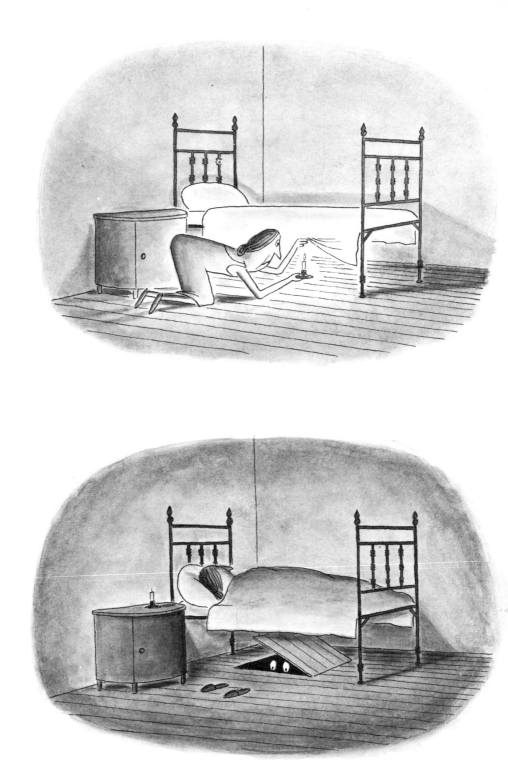

S.GROSS

S.GROSS

"Well, I guess that proves it. Seeing-eye kangaroos are not the answer."

"He followed me home, Mom. Can I eat him?"

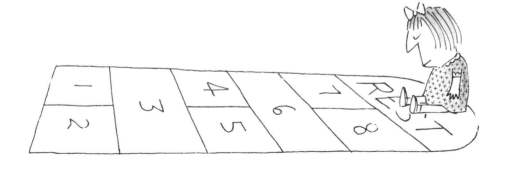

"Could you call the vet? My wife is going to have a baby!"

S.GROSS

S. GROSS

"What about some protein?"

S. GROSS

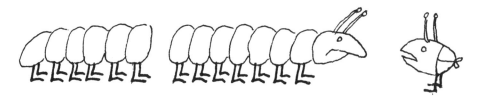

"I've decided to start my own caterpillar."

"We're a pecking order."

S.GROSS

"I'm not very hungry, Mister, but I sure could use a drink."

S.GROSS

"Congratulations, you klutz! You've just made organic matter."

GROSS

"I changed my mind. I'd rather be a big enchanted prince in a small pond than a small enchanted prince in a big pond."

S. GROSS

"Let's just stick to making pizza, Fred."

S.GROSS

S.GROSS

"For heaven's sake! Can't we do anything about these dragon flies?"

S.GROSS

"I'm from the marshall's office.
Nabisco has foreclosed on your mortgage."

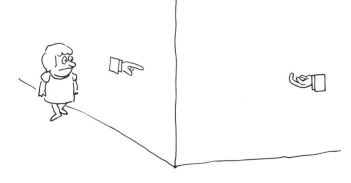

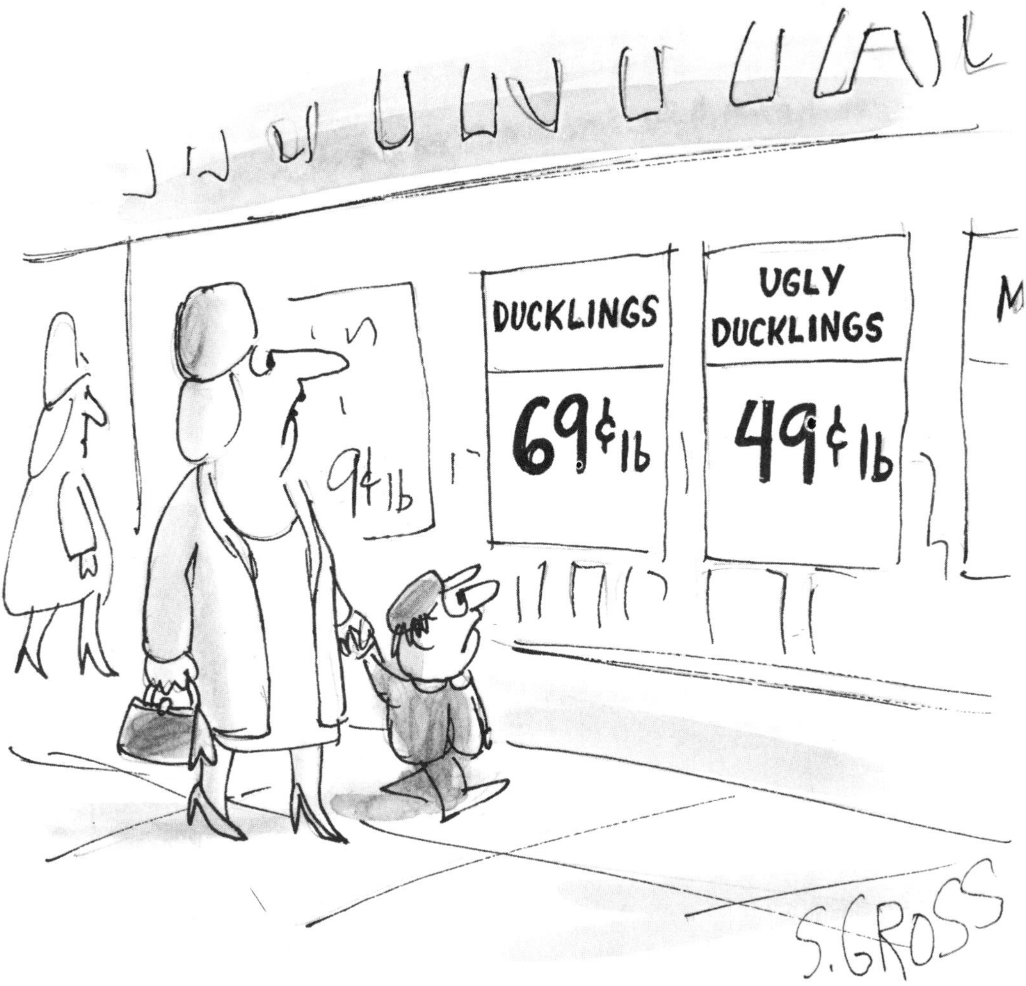
DUCKLINGS
69¢ lb
UGLY DUCKLINGS
49¢ lb
9¢ lb
S. GROSS

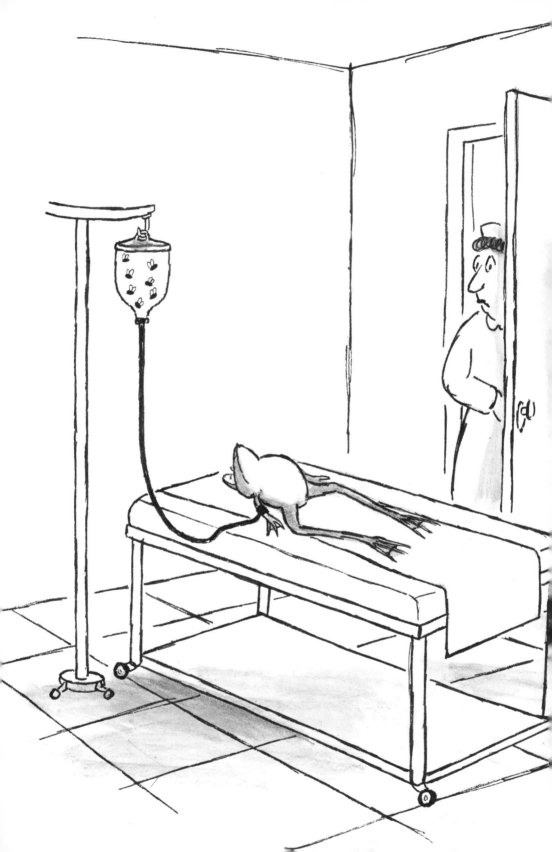

"We're moving to Sesame Street."

"I don't care if he is enchanted, you can't take a frog off as a dependent!"

"Hello, Audubon Society? . . . I want to report an obscene birdcall."

S.GRO